CAN I FIND PEACE?

Reflections on Psalm 23

NORMAN WARREN

BARBOUR

PUBLISHING, INC.

Uhrichsville, Ohio

WHERE CAN I FIND PEACE?

*Reflections on
Psalm 23*

Member of the
Evangelical Christian
Publishers Association

CONTENTS

INTRODUCTION

Y ou may be living on your own at home. You may be in a retirement home or in a hospital. Whatever your circumstances, Psalm 23 has a special message for you.

It has meant so much to countless people for literally thousands of years.

No other part of the Bible is better known and loved.

Its message of hope and love is as fresh as ever.

Let us look at it again and see perhaps in a new way how it can help us today and bring us closer to the Shepherd Himself.

PSALM 23

The LORD is my shepherd,
I shall not be in want.
He makes me lie down in green pastures,
he leads me beside quiet waters,
he restores my soul.
He guides me in paths of righteousness
for his name's sake.
Even though I walk through the valley
of the shadow of death,
I will fear no evil, for you are with me;
your rod and your staff, they comfort me.
You prepare a table before me
in the presence of my enemies.
You anoint my head with oil;
my cup overflows.
Surely goodness and love will follow me
all the days of my life,
and I will dwell in the house of the
LORD forever.

THE LORD

People have many different pictures of God. They may be childhood memories, or ideas picked up over many years.

Some may see Him as a kind old gentleman with a long white beard. Others may think of a powerful being who doesn't really care, or perhaps a ghostlike ruler of the universe.

Some people say, "There isn't a God because I can't see Him."

We cannot see the wind—but we can see it blowing the leaves in the trees.

We cannot see electricity—but we know it is there when we switch the light on.

We cannot see air—but we could not live a minute without it.

We cannot see love—but we know it is there in those who care for us.

We cannot see God. We know He is there because of the wonderful world all around us. It is full of beauty and color and amazing designs from the tiniest insect to the vast unending universe. Things do not happen by chance. Someone put it all together. This great Architect and Creator is called God.

This Creator God loves beauty and color —He has made so much.

His power is clearly seen in the great soaring mountains, in the restless sea and the vastness of space—the stars and planets and galaxies.

We all live in time. We have a beginning and an end. Because we are like this, we think God must be like it, too. But He is different.

He is eternal. He has no beginning and no end.

We change—our bodies, our habits, our friends.

God never changes. His love and care never change.

He will never let us down. He never grows old and weak.

THE SHEPHERD GOD

What is God really like?

The world of creation tells us something about God. He is far too wonderful for us to understand Him. So if we are to get to know Him, He has to make the first move.

So He decided to come in person to our earth. He came in a way we can understand. He came as a baby.

His mother was a country girl called Mary. And His name was Jesus.

He was born just as we are. He was fully human. But He was also fully God.

He was full of love and kindness, full of life and fun.

He had no streak of selfishness or wrong.

Because Jesus was human, He knows what we go through.

Because Jesus is God, He is able to help us.

Psalm 23 is all about God. And because Jesus came to show us what God is like, as the perfect Shepherd, it is all about Jesus.

He is the Lord of heaven and earth.

He is the Lord of this psalm.

I SHALL NOT BE IN WANT

*I want to know that God
accepts me as I am.
I want to know I am forgiven.*

It is so easy for people who are getting older to feel unwanted. They don't feel they are being treated as people of value. God loves us. He wants us to be His friends.

We are of such value to Him that He was willing to let Jesus die for us.

Sin and selfishness are behind all the wrong and evil. They block the way to God like a great barrier.

We cannot remove this barrier ourselves. We are not good enough. Someone had to do it for us, someone absolutely good in every way.

Jesus is the only one who has ever lived who has never done anything wrong.

He was the only one who could take away the sin that blocks the way to God.

As God He was perfect. As a person He alone was perfect.

It cost Him His life. He was put to death on that ancient form of gallows, the cross. There He carried the punishment, the death penalty for our sin—the sin that blocks the way to God.

> *There was no other good enough*
> *to pay the price of sin.*
> *He only could unlock the gate*
> *of heaven and let us in.*
> *He died that we might be forgiven,*
> *he died to make us good,*
> *that we might go at last to heaven,*
> *saved by his precious blood.*

This is how much Jesus, the Good Shepherd, loves each one of us.

THE GOD OF LOVE

How do I know God is interested in me?
How do I know He loves me?

The picture of Jesus as the Shepherd is one of loving and caring.

A shepherd knows all about his sheep. He knows them by name. Each one is precious. He feeds them and guards them. If one gets lost he goes after it, no matter the cost, until he finds it.

God knows all about us, all that has happened to us in the past, all that is happening to us now, all that is going to happen in the future.

He is aware of all our fears and troubles, all our hopes and joys.

There is nothing about us He does not know.

And He loves each of us as individuals. We are each precious to Him.

He accepts us just as we are. We don't

have to try to do good to win His love. He loved us long before we loved Him or even first heard of Him. We don't have to do religious things before God accepts us.

This is the wonder of God's love—so different from ours. As Paul was to write in the New Testament so many years after this psalm:

> *While we were still sinners,*
> *Christ died for us.*
>   ROMANS 5:8

God did not wait until we were good before sending Jesus. He knew that would never happen.

The Shepherd loved us so much that He was willing to lay down His life for us.

THE LIVING LORD

The Shepherd laid down His life for the sheep.

Jesus died. His body was put in a tomb, a great stone pushed across the entrance, and soldiers were posted to guard it.

But the amazing thing was that He came back to life. Jesus rose from death and is alive. So the Lord is my Shepherd.

On that first Easter Day the body was gone, the tomb empty.

Jesus showed Himself to His friends fully alive. All their fears and doubts vanished like a morning mist.

He had won the victory over death and over sin. The way to God was now wide open.

I shall not be in want.

Because of Jesus, God promises to forgive us all our sins, to make each one of us His own child, to take away all our guilty fears, to give us eternal life.

There is nothing in the way now to stop us from coming to know God.

GREEN PASTURES

I can't help worrying about the future.
At times I get afraid of growing older.
I can no longer do
the things I used to do.

We are all human, and growing old is part of being human. There is nothing we can do to stop this—it is part of life. Jesus our Shepherd knows this.

He makes me lie down in green pastures,
he leads me beside quiet waters.

Jesus knows all about us.

You know when I sit and when I rise;
you perceive my thoughts from afar.
You discern my going out
and my lying down;
you are familiar with all my ways.

Before a word is on my tongue
*   you know it completely, O LORD.*
                              PSALM 139:2–4

He knows we are getting old, He knows our weaknesses.

He knows we cannot get about and do what once we could.

He promises to give us His peace in our hearts.

"Come to me, all you who are weary
and burdened, and I will give you rest."
                              MATTHEW 11:28

Just as the shepherd leads his sheep into gentle pastures where there are quiet, refreshing waters, so Jesus will give us inner rest and refreshment, His own peace as we come to Him and ask Him for it.

HE LEADS ME

What is going to happen to me?
I dread being all alone.
I am so afraid I will fall over
and break my leg
and be crippled.

These thoughts and others like them will come to all of us. The older we get the stronger the thoughts may be.

None of us knows what the future holds. But Jesus knows.

He restores my soul.
He guides me in paths of righteousness
for his name's sake.

He knows exactly the whole plan of our lives. He holds the future; He has it under control. He is the Lord of the past, the present, and the future.

*Jesus Christ is the same yesterday
today and forever.*

HEBREWS 13:8

He promises not only to be with us, but to guide us, to take us by the hand and lead us into the future. And it will be the right path, the best path for us.

And I said to the man who stood at the gate of the year, "Give me a light that I may tread safely into the unknown."

And he replied, "Go out into the darkness and put your hand into the hand of God. That shall be to you better than light and safer than a known way."

MINNIE LOUISE HASKINS

VALLEY OF THE SHADOW

The very thought of death scares me.
I see my friends passing away
and wonder when it will be my turn.

Death is one appointment we must all keep. And it is very natural to fear the unknown.

But Jesus has been down into death—and come back alive. The Christian hope of life beyond the grave is real.

Even though I walk through the valley
of the shadow of death,
I will fear no evil, for you are with me;
your rod and your staff, they comfort me.

Death still remains an enemy. It is an alien in the world God originally intended. The inevitable result of sin in the world is death, the ultimate separation.

But death is a defeated enemy! Jesus has

died the death we deserve.

One day His kingdom will be complete. All the sheep will have been gathered into the flock. Then all creation will be remade. Sin and death and separation will be no more.

In the meantime, death for the believer in Jesus has been transformed into a gateway into life. Our old, wasted bodies will be no more. We will be given new bodies. A seed buried in the ground "dies"—but it grows up into a plant that will bear fruit or flowers beyond the wildest imagination of the seed!

So though we may fear death, Jesus has taken away its sting. If we have put our trust in Jesus, it is no longer up to us what will happen. We will go to be with Him.

I will fear no evil, for You are with me.

A BANQUET

I don't feel I am wanted any longer.
I don't want to be a nuisance.
I no longer feel I am of any use.

E verything about life today seems to be for the young. It is so easy as you get older to feel you don't count any more.

Worse still if you begin to feel you are just a burden, even to your family.

The scene in the psalm now changes from the shepherd with his sheep to a king giving a banquet.

You prepare a table before me
in the presence of my enemies.
You anoint my head with oil;
my cup overflows.

You are an honored guest. The king has invited you to sit close to Him.

All your enemies—your fears, worries, doubts—have been driven out and put in their place.

Jesus is the King. You are of such value to Him that He invites you to sit with Him in the place of honor.

It is true that the Christian is a servant and follower of Jesus. It is also true, as the apostle Paul said,

> *We are God's children. . . heirs of God*
> *and co-heirs with Christ.*
> ROMANS 8:16–17

The Christian is a prince or princess in God's royal family.

This is what it means when it says, "You anoint my head with oil."

With such a wonderful King, no wonder the Christian can say "my cup overflows" with joy and gratitude. And this isn't just something future, which we have to wait for heaven to enjoy.

We were made to enjoy fellowship with God here and now. And Jesus has made it possible.

THE HOUSE OF THE LORD

I long to go home. . . .
I've never had a real home. . . .

H ome. That is the final picture we are
given:

Surely goodness and love will follow me
all the days of my life,
and I will dwell in the house of the LORD
forever.

What a lovely picture it is. What is home?

Well, not just a house or a building. Home
is where you belong. Home is where you are
loved and accepted for yourself.

You don't have to play-act at home. You
can be you.

You can be real and know you will not be
rejected.

That is how Jesus describes heaven—as
home. It is where we belong: our home with

the One we love and trust.

This life is very short and passing. Time flies by so fast. We are strangers and pilgrims here.

Life can be very hard, with much pain and suffering and unhappiness. But the Good Shepherd is with us even now. His love and joy and peace can be in our hearts and minds to give us strength and courage and faith.

We can know a bit of heaven now, even among the troubles of this life. And at the end of the journey we can know a welcome waiting for us that is beyond our dreams.

Even now Jesus is preparing a glorious home for all His people. The Christian's real home is not here on earth, but in heaven.

All who love and trust Him:

- will see Him

- will be made like Him

- will be with Him—millions of people right from the very dawn of
  time.

I will dwell in the house of the LORD forever.

MY SHEPHERD

*I long to know Jesus
as my Good Shepherd.*

An actor and an elderly clergyman were having an audition for the radio to see who should do the reading of Psalm 23. They both read it. But each had a very different way of reading it. The actor turned to the clergyman and said, "There is one big difference between us. You know the Shepherd."

Do you know the Shepherd?

It is one thing to know about Jesus Christ—what He did and said. It is another thing to know Him in your life.

You may have been brought up to believe in God, but He still seems distant. Or you may not have had much opportunity to get to know about Him.

Now you want to know Him. You want to know that He loves you, accepts you, and forgives you. You want to be sure you have eternal life and will go to be with Jesus in heaven when you die.

Here are three simple steps to becoming a real believer, one who trusts Jesus:

- Admit. You cannot get to God by your own good deeds; the sheep caught in a thicket needs the shepherd to get free. You have sinned in God's sight in your thoughts, words, and actions: "We all, like sheep, have gone astray."

- Believe. Jesus died on the cross for your sins. He took the punishment you deserve because He loves you. The Shepherd laid down His life for the sheep.

- Come. Come to Him now, just as you are, and open your heart to Him. Let the Shepherd gather you into His flock, and care for you and protect you.

You become a true Christian and child of God when you put your trust in Him as your own Good Shepherd.

LOST SHEEP

At times God seems so far away.

Sometimes a sheep wanders off and gets lost. The shepherd will leave the rest of the flock and hunt for that lost sheep until he has found it.

We all, like sheep, have gone astray,
each of us has turned to his own way.
ISAIAH 53:6

All of us do things, say things, think things that we know are wrong.

None of us is perfect—we know this. And the older we get the more we know it to be so. We like to do what we want—we want our own way.

The Bible calls this sin. Even the word S-I-N has "I" in the middle. It's "me first"— "I" in the center of my life.

Sin is not just killing, stealing, and telling

lies. I sin when I do what I want, when I leave God out of my life, when I don't do things I know I should.

We are all like this. This is why there are wars and quarrels and family break-ups.

This is why God seems miles away and not to care.

Just as a quarrel cuts us off from a friend, so sin cuts us off from God.

But God did something about it.

He loved the world so much that He sent His only Son to open the way back to Him, to mend the broken friendship.

For God so loved the world that he gave his one and only Son, that whoever believes in him shall not perish but have eternal life.
JOHN 3:16

OPENING THE DOOR

You want to become a true Christian or perhaps you want to make sure that you are one. You want Jesus to be your Good Shepherd.

Find a place where you can be quiet and alone.

Think of Jesus and His love for you, dying on the cross, the terrible pain and shame, all for you. He was the Shepherd who laid down His life for the sheep.

Think of His victory over sin and death. He rose again and is alive forevermore.

Think of Him knocking at the door of your life, calling you to open the door to Him and invite Him in to be your Friend and Master. He wants to come in and share your life with you. He wants to enter into that fellowship with you for which you were created.

Now there follows a prayer.

As you pray this prayer you are opening

the door of your life to Jesus and inviting Him in.

Pray it phrase by phrase quietly, thinking carefully about what you are saying and what you are doing.

Lord Jesus Christ,
I know I have sinned against You,
in my thoughts, words, and actions.
There are so many good things I have not done.
Please forgive me.
I am sorry for my sins
and turn from all I know to be wrong.
But You are the Good Shepherd
who laid down His life for the sheep.
You gave Your life upon the cross for me.
Gratefully I give my life back to You.
Now I ask You to come into my life.
Come in as my Savior to forgive me,
come in as my Lord to control me,
come in as my Friend to be with me,
and I will be Yours
all the remaining years of my life.
Amen.

THE LORD IS
MY SHEPHERD

Y ou have said this prayer and meant every word.

You have asked Jesus Christ into your life and He has come.

You may not feel any different. Don't rely on what you feel, rely on what Jesus promises.

> *If anyone hears my voice and opens*
> *the door, I will come in.*
> REVELATION 3:20

Jesus is God: When He makes a promise He always keeps it. He now lives in you by His Holy Spirit.

> *To all who received him. . .*
> *he gave the right to become children of God.*
> JOHN 1:12

You have received Jesus into your life.

You have been reborn, born into God's family.

You are now a child of God.

"He who believes [in me] has everlasting life."
JOHN 6:47

You believe in Jesus, you have trusted your life to Him.

You now have eternal life. When you die you will go straight to be with Jesus in heaven. You have His promise.

"I am with you always, to the very end of the age."
MATTHEW 28:20

You will never be alone. Jesus is with you always, in every situation, at all times.

You also become a child in God's family. His family is the church, which consists of all who trust in Jesus, whatever their color, background, or country.

So now join up with your local church. Join the family!

And do not be afraid to share with your family and friends that Jesus is now your Shepherd, your Friend, your God. Show to the world you now belong to the Good Shepherd.

Surely goodness and love
will follow me
all the days of my life,
and I will dwell
in the house of the Lord
forever.

Inspirational Library

Beautiful purse/pocket-size editions of Christian classics boun[d]
flexible leatherette. These books make thoughtful gifts for ev[ery]
one on your list, including yourself!

When I'm on My Knees   The highly popular collection of devotional thoughts on prayer, especially for women.
>   Flexible Leatherette $4.97

The Bible Promise Book   Over 1,000 promises from God's Word arranged by topic. What does God promise about matters like: Anger, Illness, Jealousy, Love, Money, Old Age, and Mercy? Find out in this book!
>   Flexible Leatherette $3.97

Daily Wisdom for Women   A daily devotional for women seeking biblical wisdom to apply to their lives. Scripture taken from the New American Standard Version of the Bible.
>   Flexible Leatherette $4.97

My Daily Prayer Journal   Each page is dated and features a Scripture verse and ample room for you to record your thoughts, prayers, and praises. One page for each day of the year.
>   Flexible Leatherette $4.97

Available wherever books are sold.
Or order from:

Barbour Publishing, Inc.
P.O. Box 719
Uhrichsville, OH 44683
http://www.barbourbooks.com

If you order by mail, add $2.00 to your order for shipping.
Prices are subject to change without notice.